★ LEGENDARY AFRICAN AMERICANS ★

THE LIFE OF DR. CHARLES DREW

Blood Bank Innovator

Series Consultant:
Dr. Russell L. Adams, Chairman
Department of Afro-American Studies, Howard University

Anne Schraff

Enslow Publishers, Inc.
40 Industrial Road
Box 398
Berkeley Heights, NJ 07922
USA
http://www.enslow.com

Originally published as *Dr. Charles Drew: Blood Bank Innovator* in 2003.

Library of Congress Cataloging-in-Publication Data

Schraff, Anne E.
The life of Dr. Charles Drew : blood bank innovator / Anne Schraff.
pages cm. — (Legendary african americans)
Includes bibliographical references and index.
Audience: Grade 4 to 6
ISBN 978-0-7660-6265-8
1. Drew, Charles, 1904–1950—Juvenile literature. 2. African American surgeons —Juvenile literature. 3. Surgeons—United States—Biography—Juvenile literature. 4. Blood banks—United States—Juvenile literature. I. Title.
RD27.35.D74S377 2015
617.092—dc23
[B]

2014027438

Future editions:
Paperback ISBN: 978-0-7660-6266-5
EPUB ISBN: 978-0-7660-6267-2
Single-User PDF ISBN: 978-0-7660-6268-9
Multi-User PDF ISBN: 978-0-7660-6269-6

Printed in the United States of America
102014 Bang Printing, Brainerd, Minn.
10 9 8 7 6 5 4 3 2 1

To Our Readers:
We have done our best to make sure all Internet addresses in this book were active and appropriate when we went to press. However, the author and the publisher have no control over and assume no liability for the material available on those Internet sites or on other Web sites they may link to. Any comments or suggestions can be sent by e-mail to comments@enslow.com or to the address on the back cover.

♲ Enslow Publishers, Inc., is committed to printing our books on recycled paper. The paper in every book contains 10% to 30% post-consumer waste (PCW). The cover board on the outside of each book contains 100% PCW. Our goal is to do our part to help young people and the environment too!

Photo Credits: AP Photo, p. 4.

Cover Photo: AP Photo

CONTENTS

Due to Dr. Charles R. Drew's invention of the first large-scale blood storage system, millions of lives have been saved. Drew was the first director of the American Red Cross blood bank.

Chapter 1

Blood for Britain

By April 1940, World War II was underway. Many European nations had already fallen to Adolf Hitler's Germany. Now, only Great Britain stood against the German advance. In September, the air assault against Britain reduced London and the surrounding countryside to ruins. Thousands were injured and killed. The severely injured people desperately needed blood to stay alive, and at this time Britain did not have an effective way to handle blood for so many people.

The director of Britain's Army Blood Transfusion Service, John Beattie, was given the task of getting blood to the wounded. For help he turned to America's Blood Transfusion Betterment Association. Beattie asked the

Americans to ship blood from the United States to Great Britain. To coordinate this massive program, Beattie asked for one particular American doctor—Dr. Charles Drew.

Drew, a thirty-six-year-old African-American doctor, was an old friend of Beattie's. Beattie had taught Drew the science of bacteriology in medical school and had contributed to Drew's growing interest in blood research. Beattie could not imagine a more suitable man to head this life-saving program.

"Suggest you appoint overall director if program is to continue," Beattie wired America. "Suggest Charles R. Drew."[1]

Not long before this, Drew had written a thesis titled "Banked Blood," and many people believed it was "the most authoritative document to date" on the preservation of whole blood.[2] Drew had compiled all the existing knowledge he could find and added the results of his own research.[3]

At that time, many people saw black doctors as capable of treating patients of their own race, primarily for less serious illnesses, but believed these doctors lacked real intellectual ability. "This attitude I should like to change," Drew wrote.[4]

Drew took a leave of absence from his position at Howard University in Washington, D.C., and quickly set in motion the Blood for Britain project. Radio advertisements called for blood donors, and eight hospitals in New York City were linked to a central office in Manhattan. A dozen telephone operators sat around a table taking calls from people volunteering to give blood. The operators looked at maps of the city, and each donor was quickly routed to the nearest hospital. There, after a physical examination to determine the health of the donor, a pint of blood was collected. The hospital's laboratory used a centrifuge, a rotating machine to separate the blood plasma from the red blood cells. Samples were tested for the presence of bacteria, and if found pure, were placed in glass bottles to be sent to a refrigerated warehouse for shipment to Britain by the Red Cross and the military.

Plasma was very vulnerable to bacteria during storage, so Drew repeatedly tested it to ensure safety. The smallest contamination could kill a patient, leading the British to describe plasma as "liquid dynamite."[5] To guarantee safety, Drew insisted on detailed procedures every step of the way. His excellent quality control prompted DeWitt Stetten, chairman of the Blood Transfusion Betterment Association, to say "Since Drew has been in charge, our major troubles have vanished."[6]

Blood plasma was used instead of whole blood because it was cheaper to produce, could be stored for much longer periods, did not have to be typed, and there was less risk to patients receiving it.

New Yorkers by the thousands responded as never before to the appeals of Blood for Britain, eventually donating enough blood to produce fifty-five hundred vials of plasma.

Sadly, in spite of Drew's success in collecting and sending so much safe plasma to Britain, the directors of America's Blood for Britain program made a shameful decision. They would accept blood from black donors, but it had to be labeled as such before being shipped to Britain. Where this blood labeled from black donors went is not known.

By January 1941, the British had their own plasma program up and running. They no longer needed American plasma. But during the grim fall of 1940, Drew's masterful leadership and expertise saved the lives of uncounted men, women, and children.[7]

Chapter 2

Foggy Bottom Beginnings

In a spacious sixteen-room home owned by his mother's parents, Charles Richard Drew was born on June 3, 1904. The home at 1806 E Street N.W. in Washington, D.C., was located in an area nicknamed Foggy Bottom because mists rose regularly from the nearby Potomac River.

The neighborhood was mostly black, but many whites lived there, too. Shopkeepers tended to be Irish, Italian, French, and Jewish. In the Washington of this time, racial segregation was the strict order of the day. All places of entertainment, hotels, restaurants, and schools were segregated by race. At the foot of the Washington Monument, black children had their own swimming pool, and only one theater in the area was open to both races.

Charles was the first child born to Richard Thomas Drew and Nora Rosella Burrell Drew. A second child, Elsie, was born in 1906. Joseph followed in 1909, and Nora in 1913. The fifth and last child, Eva, was born in 1921.

Richard Thomas Drew was a carpet layer. Like most men of the time, he had not finished high school. He worked for the Moses Furniture Company and he became the only black member of the Carpet, Linoleum, and Soft Tile Layers Union. A red-haired, freckled man, Richard Drew grew a mustache to cover a scar on his lip from a boxing match he had engaged in for sport. He was a gentle man, devoted to his family. He enjoyed swimming, baseball, and barbering. He belonged to a barbershop quartet, the Highwarden Quartet, which often performed in riverboats along the Potomac River.

Charles's mother, Nora Drew, had graduated from Howard University with a degree in pedagogy—the art of teaching school. She was an outgoing, strong-willed woman who shared her husband's belief that the father of the family earns the living and the mother takes care of the children and the home. So, even though she was qualified to teach and could have gotten a position, she chose to devote all her time to her family and volunteer work.

Both Richard and Nora Drew were very active in the Nineteenth Street Baptist Church, an old African-American church established fifty years earlier. It was a very strong influence on the black families of the area. Richard Drew was musical director of the choir and Nora Drew was on the Board of Trustees for the church. As a young woman in Virginia, Nora Burrell had established the first black Young Men's Christian Association (YMCA) to give black youth in the region a chance at sports and character building activities.

The Drews lived with Richard Drew's parents until the birth of their first child. With Charles on the way, they moved into the large home of Nora Drew's parents and the baby boy was delivered in the Burrell home by the family doctor, Charles Marshall.

The Drews were not members of the upper-class black community in Washington, D.C., nor were they terribly poor like many other black people in the city. "We had enough," Joseph Drew later recalled. "We lived well."[1] Though racial discrimination and evidence of prejudice was all around them, the Drews managed to overcome this. "We lived in our own little world," Joseph Drew recalled.[2]

The Drew family was close-knit and supportive of all its members. The Drews came from Charlottesville, Virginia. Charles Drew's great-grandfather was a barber and a free black man in the middle 1800s. The Burrells came from Upperville, Virginia. Both Charles Drew's parents immigrated to Washington, D.C., as young adults in search of more opportunities than they could find in their native Virginia.

Both of Charles Drew's parents were very fair skinned. Research into the family yields several different nationalities and races. Charles Drew descended not only from African Americans, but also from English, Scots, Irish and Native Americans.

In the 1910 United States census, the Drews were described as Negro Americans, and that was how they saw themselves. When it was time to send their children to school or to use a community swimming pool, there was never any doubt where they would go. They would use the facilities designated for black people. When Richard Drew began teaching his children to swim, he avoided the white pools and often used the gravel barges on the Potomac as diving boards. Father and children would splash into the river from the barges. At other times they used the pools open to black people.

Although Richard Drew did not finish high school, he had great respect for education and both he and his wife conducted Sunday Bible class including readings and prayers for their children. Richard Drew often took his children on personally guided tours of the important historical monuments in Washington, explaining to them the significance of each one. The Drew children were expected to read serious books, such as works by Shakespeare and other classics.

The Drews had high expectations for their children in every respect. They were supposed to study and do well in school and also do their chores around the house. All the children, both boys and girls, learned to sew so they could keep their clothing in good condition. Young Charles's skill with the needle as he mended his shirts and trousers served him well later in life when he became a surgeon.

The Drew family was comfortable and loving. The father, as head of the family, was held up for respect. Charles Drew's mother never tired of reminding the children to respect their father because "you were cared for and educated by your father on his knee."[3] The elder Drew, as a carpet layer, spent most of his life kneeling on floors while he laid tile and carpet.

Washington, D.C., had a segregated school system and, as in most other places, the black schools received less financial support than the white schools did. Supplies were not so plentiful and classes were larger, but in spite of that, the schools were excellent. Most blacks-only schools in other parts of the country gave the children an inferior education. The black pupils found themselves poorly prepared to compete in a world that was not only prejudiced but demanded higher standards than they had learned. The black schools of Washington, though, trained their children well with a staff of skilled and dedicated teachers.

Young Charles attended Stevens Elementary School, but after a short time he transferred to Briggs Elementary. At Stevens, his love for swimming had blossomed and he was soon winning medals in competition. When Charles was eight years old, the Twelfth Street Branch of the Young Men's Christian Association, the nation's first black YMCA, opened a gymnasium pool for African-American children. Charles competed in many races, usually winning. Stevens Elementary School also had baseball and basketball teams, and Charles was good enough to play in their championship games. Here his lifelong love of sports was nurtured, though athletics never became a passion with him.

In 1917, when Charles was twelve years old, he started selling newspapers from street corners. He sold the *Washington Times* and *Herald* and the *Evening Star*. Charles discovered that his best customers were people coming from offices and factories in the area, so he became an entrepreneur in the newspaper business. He recruited six to ten other boys and stationed them at places where workers, eager for newspapers, came onto the street. By collecting a small percentage of his crew's profits and through his own corner, Charles made a tidy sum for himself. Always energetic, young Charles also got jobs at playgrounds and at construction sites doing chores for the laborers.

In the spring of 1918, fourteen-year-old Charles entered Paul Laurence Dunbar High School (named for Paul Laurence Dunbar, a gifted black poet who died in 1906 at the age of thirty-four). By all accounts, it had a fine academic record. The stately-looking five-story brick building contained one hundred and ten rooms. It was considered the best black college preparatory school in the United States. Excellent teachers set high standards for the students. The teachers at Dunbar were graduates of some of the most prestigious colleges in America, including Harvard, Oberlin, and Amherst.

Class sizes at Dunbar were small, and the curriculum stressed classical learning. Students were required to learn Latin and some Greek. Many of Dunbar's graduates went on to become famous Americans. Among them were Robert C. Weaver, who became Secretary of Housing and Urban Development, Benjamin O. Davis, the first black brigadier general in the United States Army, and William Hastie, the first black district court judge in the country.

At Dunbar, Charles achieved high grades in science and mathematics, and he was very active in sports. He lettered in four sports: football, basketball, track, and swimming. He received awards as best athlete and most popular student, and he also belonged to the Cadet Corps, serving as Captain of Company B, Third Regiment. Though playing sports never was a career possibility for Charles, he saw athletics as a major force in helping young people prepare for the challenges of life. He enjoyed the competition and the sportsmanship that athletics offered. Later, as an adult, Charles Drew was fond of pointing out how closely sports parallel life. Athletes learn to face many different situations, including disappointment, pain, and triumph—all part of life—and if they can win gracefully and lose without bitterness, they have an edge on being a successful human beings.[4]

As a teenager and as an adult, Charles loved and admired his parents. He had a special bond with his mother. As a baby he cried a lot and she became extra attentive toward him. As he grew older, her warm support was an important sustaining force in his life. Charles had a warm and friendly relationship with his father, too.

Charles's sister, Nora, recalled her brother as a "happy person, popular and outgoing."[5] As a teenager he was "confident," had a good "sense of humor" and was an "inspiring" leader to his classmates.[6] His fellow students at Dunbar voted him the "student who has done most for the school."[7]

While working hard at Dunbar, Charles also had a very difficult and demanding job at a glass factory, where he put in long hours under terrible conditions. Once, during the glass-making process, he was burned, losing all the hair on his head. Fortunately the hair grew back. Charles was willing to take almost any job to earn extra money for college. He knew that his family could barely meet the obligations of daily living and could not pay for his college expenses.

Under Charles Drew's photograph in the Dunbar High School yearbook in his senior year he is described as "ambitious, popular, athletic, sturdy." The quotation he chose was "You can do anything you think you can."[8]

Charles was awarded the James E. Walker Medal for athletic excellence at Dunbar and this led to his being offered an athletic scholarship to Amherst College for his overall abilities, not for one particular sport.

During Charles's senior year at Dunbar, tragedy struck the family. Twelve-year-old Elsie, Charles's sister, died during the 1918–1919 influenza epidemic that was sweeping the United States and parts of Europe. Elsie was already ailing with tuberculosis, but it was the influenza that took her life. The girl's death had a profound effect on Charles. Later he would call it a turning point in his life for helping him decide on his future career.

During Charles's high school years, the family moved from the grandparents's home to their own home, a two-story framed house at 2505 First Street in Arlington, Virginia. It was an all-black neighborhood of well-kept homes. In Arlington, as had been the case in Washington, D.C., strict segregation prevailed.

With high school behind him, eighteen-year-old Charles Drew left the security of the family home and the warm neighborhood and set out for the white world of Amherst College in Massachusetts.

Chapter 3

THE CALLING

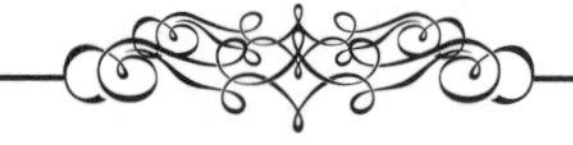

Charles Richard Drew was about six feet tall and weighed around one hundred and ninety five pounds when he entered college. He was a solidly built, handsome young man, one of the freshman class in 1922 at Amherst College in western Massachusetts. Because of his mixed ancestry he had reddish skin and hair, which earned him the nickname "Big Red." His brown eyes were small and bright. He was a soft-spoken, serious young man who fit in well with the upper-class atmosphere of Amherst College.

The student body at Amherst consisted of six hundred students, of which thirteen were black. The regular college fraternities at Amherst did not accept black students, so

Drew joined the black college fraternity Omega Psi Phi, and he became the author of the fraternity hymn. Charles Drew enjoyed music, and while he never became the musician his father was, he did play the saxophone and sing. Because of his father's interest in music, Drew knew a great deal about melodies and tones.

Drew's close friends at Amherst were other black students. He felt more at home with them than he did with his white peers. Drew called his black friends by their first names, but he addressed all other people, including the white students and both black and white strangers formally. Drew never felt an easy familiarity with people he did not know well.

Drew was attending Amherst on a general athletic scholarship and he did not disappoint. As a freshman he won a major letter in track, and as a sophomore he was an outstanding halfback on the football team. By his junior year he had won the Thomas W. Ashley Memorial Trophy as the class member who had made the greatest contribution to Amherst athletics.

In the 1925 championship game between Amherst College and Wesleyan College, Drew made a thirty-five-yard touchdown pass to win the biggest game of the year. While at Amherst, Drew was coached by D. C. "Tuss" McLaughry, who became a great admirer of young Drew. McLaughry said of Drew, "As a football player, Drew was great."[1]

Since Drew was participating in sports so heavily, he had to work hard to maintain his good grades.[2] He had entered Amherst with a strong inclination toward a career in medicine and he would need excellent grades.

In an almost exclusively white environment for the first time in his life, Drew began to feel the pain of racial prejudice as he had never felt it before. One incident stood out as especially bitter. The track team, including Drew, had gone to Brown University in Providence, Rhode Island, for a meet. After the meet was over, the Amherst team was supposed to eat together at a fine nearby hotel, the Narragansett. However, before the team left for the feast at the hotel, Drew and three other black players were taken aside and told that because the Narragansett Hotel refused to serve black people, they would have to eat their meal at the Brown University commons. The angry black athletes watched their white teammates board the bus for the hotel. Drew himself never forgot the slight.[3]

The track meet incident was not the exception, but rather the rule at Amherst. When Amherst's football team played Princeton, the players were told that Princeton fans were well known for their rude and ugly behavior toward black players from visiting teams. One of Drew's teammates was very dark skinned, and he was subject to screamed taunts from the Princeton fans. When the fans learned that the ruddy-skinned Drew was also an African American, they jeered at him and cheered wildly when he was spilled upside down by a Princeton player.

The glee club at Amherst refused to accept black students as well. When the club traveled, the members stayed in the homes of alumni, all white, and the school did not want to risk offending the alumni by bringing a black student to their homes.

Probably one of the saddest instances of prejudice occurred when the captain of the Amherst football team was to be chosen. By tradition, the most successful third-year man on the football team was elected captain in his senior year. Drew, outstanding in football and track, was the natural choice. But he was denied the honor because of his race.

As one of Amherst's outstanding seniors, Drew was also eligible for membership in the Scarab Club, an elite social and academic club. But the student members of the club rejected his membership. In this case, however, a number of white students resigned in protest from the Scarab Club because they knew and liked Drew.

In spite of the racial slights, Drew made the most of his education at Amherst. It was a fine school and he made many friends there, some of whom remained close for life. William H. Hastie, Drew's old friend from Dunbar was there, and Drew made friends with Ben Davis, who later became a New York City councilman.

Drew dealt with racism at Amherst the way he would deal with it throughout his life. He made up his mind to excel in areas where race was not a barrier. When he met the goals he set for himself, he believed he was not only frustrating his prejudiced white colleagues, he was also paving the way for black people who came after him. Drew was always conscious of his role as pathfinder, smoothing the trail for those who followed.

In 1926, Drew graduated from Amherst College. By this time he was certain that he wanted to be a doctor. What had always pointed him in this direction was the death of his sister, Elsie. He wrote that, at the time when his sister and hundreds of others were dying of influenza, he was saddened by the inability of medicine to stop the disease. "I have studied the sciences diligently since that time," he recalled.[4]

But there were other motives as well that led Charles Drew into medicine. During his junior year at Amherst, he injured his leg playing football. The spike of the opponent's shoe cut his thigh. When an infection set in, Drew was hospitalized. During the time he spent at the hospital he was able to observe the medical staff at work. He became interested in the details of how the body works and medical procedures for healing.

Once Drew decided to pursue a career in medicine, he proceeded with single-minded energy. He never hesitated or questioned his choice. But money was a major problem. Medical school was expensive, and the Drews were still raising younger children. Joseph was seventeen, Nora was thirteen, and Eva was five. The Drews, though comfortable, were never wealthy and they could not help their son achieve his expensive dream of medical school. Drew realized that if he was to become a doctor, he would have to find the money himself.

Charles Drew secured jobs as director of athletics at Morgan College in Baltimore, Maryland, and as a biology and chemistry instructor there. Founded in 1869 to prepare black men to be Christian ministers, Morgan had evolved into a general liberal arts college. Drew worked at Morgan College for two years, living on a tight budget and saving every penny he could for his future education. He coached the football and basketball teams and, during the summer, he earned additional money teaching children to swim at Baltimore's public pools.

As a teacher at Morgan College, Drew displayed qualities that would mark his entire life. He had the ability to reach students, even those with modest talents, and to inspire them to do their very best.

It was Drew's strong hope that he could train as a medical doctor at Howard University. He would then be able to live at home, saving the expenses of a dorm or an apartment. Drew loved his family and he welcomed the chance to be close to them again, and he had great respect for Howard University. But, to Drew's shock, he was rejected by Howard University because he was short two English credits from his courses at Amherst College. In a rare display of anger, Drew vowed he would one day return to Howard and run the place.[5]

Now Charles Drew had to look elsewhere for the training he needed to become a doctor.

Chapter 4

North to Canada

Charles Drew applied to McGill University Medical School in Montreal, Canada, and was accepted. He left the United States for Canada in the fall of 1928.

As a medical student, Drew remained active in sports. While at McGill, he won the Canadian championships in the high and low hurdles and also in the high jump and broad jump. He was also an outstanding student.[1]

But money continued to be a serious problem for the young medical student. He got a job as a waiter in the McGill University dining room, but even this did not meet his tuition and living costs. When he discussed his problems with his old football coach, Tuss McLaughry, the coach raised several hundred dollars from among Drew's friends at Amherst. This tided Drew over during his freshman year.

For most of his time at McGill however, Drew was struggling financially. He rented a room with an Irish family in Montreal, paying $20 a month. He had little or nothing let over for extras. Sometimes his friends, feeling sorry for him, would try to pay his way at social events, but he always refused. It was a matter of pride for him.

Drew's poverty and loneliness reached a very low point in early 1930. It was New Year's Day and Drew was walking down the Montreal street. He stopped for tea and toast at the Northeastern Lunchroom and used up most of his funds. He had just a dollar left and he needed that for food the next day. He continued walking, not sure what he hoped to find.

"Excitement maybe," Drew wrote in an eight page composition dated 12:30 A.M. January 1, 1930. "[Or] trouble—most anything out of the ordinary."[2]

The twenty-six-year-old Drew watched merry young couples celebrating New Year's Eve on the streets of Montreal. He wanted to join the party but he had no money. He wrote of his hopes of finding a nice girlfriend with brown eyes that had a "merry twinkle," or black eyes "that intrigue," or indeed, "any kind of eyes."[3]

In the fall of 1930, Charles Drew's financial hardship was relieved when he received one thousand dollars from the Julius Rosenwald Fund. The scholarship was established in 1917 by Rosenwald, a Chicago businessman and philanthropist, to build schools for poor children in rural areas, and then later to grant scholarships to promising young black students. Benefiting from these scholarships were many successful black students, including the famous photographer Gordon Parks.

Drew was given the Williams Prize for academic excellence in his senior year at McGill. The prize was based on the results of a test given to the five best members of the graduating class.

When he came to McGill, Charles Drew had his first experience living in a society where the color lines were not so strictly drawn as they were in the United States. He was selected to join Alpha Omega Alpha, the honorary scholarship fraternity for medical students. It was not a black fraternity as his former one in the United States was, but instead one that looked only at academic excellence.

Charles Drew was no longer contending with a segregated society. Here he could mix with white people in social situations. There were no businesses or places of recreation in Canada limited to whites only. Drew thrived in this more tolerant racial atmosphere. He began making good white friends like Richard B. Dunn, who later became a North Carolina gynecologist.

Dunn and Drew frequented the favorite student hangouts together, like Kaufmans, whose specialty of the house was pigs knuckles. Fifty years after they had gone to medical school together, Dunn recalled Drew as "charming, cheerful, and delightful."[4]

At McGill, Drew also became friends with Dr. John Beattie, who was a young British professor of bacteriology. Beattie was slightly older than Drew, and he was temporarily in Canada. Later he returned to Great Britain and eventually became director of the Royal College of Surgeons. His friendship with Beattie was to become very crucial to Richard Drew's medical career.

While a student at McGill, Drew received distressing news from home. The severe economic depression that had crippled Europe and now devastated the economy of the United States had hit home. Many men were being laid off and middle-class families with little or no savings were especially hard hit. Charles Drew's father was laid off from the carpet and tile laying job that he had raised his family on. There was not only the economic impact but also the serious blow to Richard Drew's pride. He spent his days sitting in the park, reading the few want-ads that appeared in the classified section, and unsuccessfully applying for work. It became necessary for Charles Drew to take money from his own meager funds and send it home to his family.

In 1933, Charles Drew graduated from McGill Medical School, second in a class of one hundred and thirty seven students. He now had a medical doctor degree, known at McGill as a M.D.C.M. (doctor of medicine) as well as a master of chirurgie (surgery) degree. Doctors graduating from McGill University did their one-year internship at the Royal Victoria Hospital and Montreal General Hospital. During 1933 and 1934, Drew worked at both hospitals. He did his primary internship at Royal Victoria Hospital and a rotating internship at Montreal General Hospital. The following year Drew became a resident (doctor-in-training) at Montreal General Hospital.

In response to receiving the Rosenwald Scholarship, Drew wrote a gracious letter of appreciation which gave his reasons for choosing a career in medicine. Written in 1930, the letter outlined the young doctor's goals as he began practicing. In the letter he told how his interest in medicine had blossomed into something very powerful. He said his dream was to "prevent or cure disease, alleviate suffering," and "give men a chance to live."[5]

The year 1935 was a traumatic one for Charles Drew. He received word that his father, Richard Thomas Drew, had died at age fifty-seven of pneumonia. Charles Drew returned at once to be with his family. His sister, Nora, and his brother, Joseph, were now teachers, but fourteen-year-old Eva was still in school. Richard Drew was buried at the Nineteenth Street Baptist Church where he had sung in the choir.

Charles Drew applied to hospital training programs, called residencies, all over the United States. Young doctors need to go through the residency process before going into the practice of medicine. During residency, they work at a hospital under doctor-teachers. Drew, however, could not get a residency.

One of Drew's applications went to Mayo University at Rochester, New York. When he was not accepted it was especially painful for him because he wanted to do his surgical training there. The reasons for his rejection were not given to him, but many years later another doctor explained why Drew could not get into any of the big-name institutions in the United States. Dr. Allen O. Whipple, head of the Department of Surgery at Columbia University, told Drew that someone of his racial background might not be able to win the confidence of the wealthy white people who used these hospitals.[6]

Charles Drew turned to Howard University, which now had its first black president, Mordecai Johnson. Johnson had already heard of Drew and was interested in him, so when Drew applied there he was immediately accepted.

Howard University had been founded in 1867 to train black teachers and ministers to guide and teach slaves freed after the Civil War, as well as twenty-five-thousand free-born black people. It was first called Howard Normal and Theological Institute. It was named for General Oliver Otis Howard, one of the founding members of the

Freedmen Bureau, a government agency to help former slaves adjust to their new freedom. Howard had always been run by white men, but now it finally had a black president and control of the school was passing into the hands of black scholars.

Drew was hired as an assistant instructor in pathology for the 1935–1936 year. He would earn $150 a month.

Chapter 5

HOWARD AND FREEDMEN'S— A NEW ERA

Charles Drew was entering Howard University Medical School as an instructor at a time when the whole school was changing. Howard University, with its second-rate department, was struggling under strong new leadership to become a nationally recognized place of distinction. Over the next few years, Dr. Mordecai Johnson, who had come to the school as president in 1926, would triple the faculty, double their salaries, and train half the black physicians graduating in the entire United States.[1]

Howard University trained its physicians at Freedmen's Hospital. Many of the hospital buildings had been built at the turn of the century and were badly in need of repair.

The federal government supported the hospital but the funds were undependable. Freedmen's Hospital lacked current medical equipment, even though it was the major health facility for most of Washington's black population. The hospital was extremely overcrowded and there were ongoing sanitation problems. Still, because it was the only hospital in the United States where a black physician was sure he could get training, its importance was great.

A few white colleges might admit one or two black physicians for training, but in general no graduating black doctor was assured of a place except at Howard. Unfortunately, because of the awareness that Freedmen's Hospital was underfunded and had many problems, the prestige of a doctor getting his training there was lowered. This added to the already widespread view that black doctors were not as good as white doctors. Some thought black doctors could not treat serious illnesses and were only good for dispensing remedies in small country towns.

When Charles Drew entered the program at Howard, he was part of the team that would change this thinking. An energetic new dean of Howard Medical School was appointed—Numa P. G. Adams. His goal was to raise Howard's standards and to train and support excellent new black doctors. Drew became assistant in surgery at Freedmen's Hospital for the 1936–1937 year and a resident in surgery at Howard Medical School. In the 1937–1938 year, Drew advanced to instructor in surgery. Dean Adams saw in Drew just the sort of man he was looking for to help bring excellence to Howard University Medical School and Freedmen's Hospital.

The way to equip the black physicians at Howard with the skills to make them the best was to give them specialty training at well respected medical schools. They could then return to Howard with shining credentials, putting the reputation of the school on a par with white schools. Dean Adams was always on the lookout for young black physicians who seemed capable of reaching the highest level of excellence and Charles Drew was one of them.

Dean Adams wanted Drew to get his doctor of science degree, so he recommended him for a Rockefeller Fellowship in 1938. Drew was accepted for two years of graduate study under Dr. Allen O. Whipple at Columbia University Medical School and Presbyterian Hospital. Whipple was widely regarded as a great surgeon and Drew was getting the opportunity of a lifetime to work with him. Drew's direct supervisor was Dr. John Scudder, assistant professor of clinical surgery and a researcher working with fluid balance, blood chemistry, and blood transfusion. Fluid balance was the careful monitoring of a patient during the transfusion of blood. Drew was already interested in blood research, so the assignment was perfect for him. While at Columbia, Drew would be working toward the advanced degree of doctor of science in medicine.

Charles Drew moved to Columbia University in New York and when there was a vacancy in the medical school, he was appointed to the resident staff at Columbia Presbyterian Hospital. For the next year and a half, Drew was a surgeon-in-training in one of the nation's finest research and teaching hospitals.

Drew was breaking new ground at Columbia Presbyterian Hospital, but it was not easy. No black resident had ever been trained here before. Although the hospital had been established to treat the poor of New York—many of whom were black—black doctors were not allowed to treat patients.

Charles Drew, though welcomed as a student at Columbia University Medical School, was supposed to stay out of sight and work in the laboratory. He was not to care for patients—even those of his own race. But Presbyterian Hospital was dealing with a very extraordinary man. Drew's charismatic personality once again enabled him to jump over great hurdles. As anatomist W. Montague Cobb, who knew Drew at Howard University, later recalled, Drew was "popular wherever he went."[2]

Dr. Whipple was drawn to Drew's magnetic personality as well, so even though black doctors were not allowed to enter the wards of Presbyterian Hospital and treat patients, when Whipple made his rounds, Drew was often with him. Officially Drew was not caring for patients, but he did so unofficially all the time.[3] It was not until the late

1940s that black doctors gained official staff privileges in some white hospitals and far later than that in many other hospitals.

Helping Drew's cause was the fact that he was light-skinned. Many patients thought he was white. A doctor with darker skin would have had much greater problems. However, Drew's primary weapon against the racism of the hospital was his appealing personality.

One incident illustrates just how successful Drew was in breaking down racial barriers. Since there never had been a black resident at Presbyterian Hospital, there were no whites-only rules for the staff dining room. However, realizing that his presence might cause problems, Drew ate alone outside the dining area. Noticing this, some of the other doctors asked their colleagues if Drew would be welcome in the dining room. One doctor, Octo Lee, was from Mississippi, where the color lines were drawn very strictly. Lee said he was offended that a question would even be raised about whether Charles Drew was welcome in the dining room. Lee said that he and the other white doctors had already been harmed by being "denied the pleasure of having their meals with Charlie [Drew]."[4]

Drew was a tireless worker at whatever he did and during his time at Columbia he did far more than an average person would have. He drove himself very hard, working long hours so he might absorb as much of this marvelous learning experience as he could.

In 1939, Charles Drew's mother was aware that her eldest son was rising very quickly in the medical community, but she was worried that he did not yet have a wife. At thirty-five, it seemed to his mother, a man should be married. Drew was making a modest salary and, although he lived a frugal life, supporting a family would be difficult. Still, the bachelor doctor was about to please his mother and himself by ending his single life.

Chapter 6

Meeting Minnie Lenore Robbins

Back in 1930, Charles Drew suffered through a lonely New Year's Eve, longing for companionship. As he watched happy couples celebrating the coming New Year, he felt his own loneliness even more keenly. Now, nine years later, there was still no evidence that the busy doctor was having much of a social life. All he did was work and study. But in the spring of 1939, that was about to change.

As he first settled into Columbia University, Drew had a frantic schedule. Now he had a little more time. He had been asked to participate in the annual clinic at the John A. Andrew Memorial Hospital in Tuskegee, Alabama. Every year free medical clinics were held there for the poor rural black people of Alabama, Florida, Georgia, Louisiana, and Mississippi. Doctors from all over the northeastern United States came to Tuskegee, mostly black doctors from Howard University. They came to care for those who had no other access to medical treatment.

Drew was eager to participate in the Tuskegee clinic because he wanted to help his own people and he looked forward to the opportunity to meet other black doctors. On the way from New York to Alabama, Drew stopped in Atlanta to visit some childhood friends. While visiting his friends at Spelman College dining hall, Drew noticed a very pretty young woman standing nearby. When he asked about her, he was told she was Minnie Lenore Robbins, a home economics teacher at Spelman College. The twenty-eight-year-old Robbins was from Philadelphia and had been a student at Cheyney State College in Cheyney, Pennsylvania, before transferring to Spelman, where she now taught. As Drew looked at the attractive woman, she also noticed him, but, at least at first, she was not as taken with him as he was with her. Drew's friends helped him along by inviting Robbins to a party they were giving, one Drew would also be attending. At the party Drew and Robbins became very friendly and they danced together.

Drew went on to the clinic in Tuskegee and fulfilled his commitments there, but Robbins was clearly in the forefront of his mind. He had come to Tuskegee with three friends, but on the way home he broke from the party and detoured to Atlanta by train. He went at once in search of Lenore Robbins.

It was one o'clock in the morning when Charles Drew arrived at the dormitory of Spelman College. He roused the head of the dorm and asked to see Robbins. The woman refused because of the early hour of the morning, but Drew was so persistent that she finally relented and sent Robbins downstairs to meet the early-morning visitor.

Charles Drew had first met Lenore Robbins just three days earlier, but now he spoke with her for a long time and eventually proposed marriage to her. An understandably startled Robbins did not accept the marriage proposal, but she did agree to see Drew again and promised him that if everything turned out well during their courtship, it was possible that she would marry him.

Drew returned to New York and his demanding work at Columbia University and Presbyterian Hospital, and Robbins continued teaching at Spelman College. Drew immediately began a letter-writing campaign designed to win Robbins over.

In recalling Lenore Robbins years later, Dr. Asa Yancey described her as "one of the most striking, vivacious, and beautiful girls" at Spelman College.[1] She had certainly captured Drew's heart and in every spare moment he had, he wrote to her.

The first of Drew's letters arrived at Robbin's home in Atlanta only a few days after their early morning meeting at Spelman College. Drew described the deep joy he felt since meeting Lenore. He told her that because of his feelings for her, he now saw the world through "rose colored glasses," and he closed the letter with the words, "I love you."[2]

Since Drew was busy all day and late into the night doing research and making his rounds at Presbyterian Hospital, he usually wrote to Robbins in the early hours of the morning right after he got home. On April 13, 1939, he wrote to her describing a concert he had just attended that had moved him deeply. He had seen Marian Anderson sing at the Lincoln Memorial in Washington, D.C. Anderson was a famous black contralto who had sung in all the great cities of Europe. Her voice was, in the words of famed conductor Arturo Toscanini, one "heard only once in a hundred years."[3] Anderson had been scheduled to sing at Constitution Hall, but the Daughters of the American Revolution would not allow the hall to be used by a black singer. Instead, the concert was moved to the steps of the Lincoln Memorial, where Anderson sang on Easter Sunday morning. Drew was so touched by the performance that he wrote to Robbins that Anderson's music had lifted him up.

The diligent, scientific mind of Charles Drew gave way to a different kind of personality during his courtship of Lenore Robbins. His letters to her were romantic and filled with boyish enthusiasm. They often contained lines from famous poetry. One of his letters included the Elizabeth Barrett Browning poem 'How Do I Love Thee?' with every stanza copied in Drew's hand. At other times Drew himself composed the poetry he used to impress Robbins.

Lenore Robbins wrote back to her suitor with more practical letters, and once she raised questions about Drew's suitability as a husband. He responded with the plaintive suggestion that "Really, I think I have possibilities."[4]

There is no doubt that just as Drew fell immediately in love with Robbins, she also noticed something in this man that was different from anyone else she had ever known. She later wrote that when she first saw him he seemed to be someone who hailed from "a more old-fashioned and courtly time and place."[5]

Drew invited Robbins to come visit him in New York, but she resisted the suggestion for a while. He was so heavily burdened with responsibilities at the time that he could not visit her in Atlanta. Robbins finally gave in and Drew joyfully made plans to take her to the New York World's Fair. He was anxious for her to meet the family he so loved and admired. Even before Robbins arrived, Drew wrote to her describing his family, telling her about his brother, Joseph, who was in bad humor after recently falling off a roof, and his little sister, who was learning to jitterbug. Drew concluded the letter about his family lovingly saying, "I think they're pretty swell."[6]

Since the death of Drew's father, the family revolved around their mother and she had become the center of all family plans. While Drew's father was alive, his mother had been willing to let him rule, but now she took strong command.

Drew confided many deep set feelings in his letters to Lenore Robbins, telling her how lonely he had been and how much it meant to him to be himself with her. In spite of his busy schedule, he snatched time out for a Wagner concert, a ballet, and a heavyweight championship bout between Joe Louis and Tony Galento. He wrote to Robbins about all these experiences and told her how proud he was of the gentlemanly way that the black champion, Louis, acted during and after the fight.

On September 23, 1939, just five months after they had first met, Minnie Lenore Robbins and Charles Richard Drew were married. They rented an apartment at 250 West 150th Street in New York which they shared with another couple. The rent was $100 a month, with each couple sharing the cost. For someone earning as modest a salary as Drew, the arrangement was necessary.

For a short time Lenore Drew worked as a laboratory assistant to supplement the family income, but she was soon pregnant with their first child. In the summer of 1940, daughter Roberta was born. She was nicknamed Bebe, for blood bank, the work that Drew was involved in.

Charles Drew was deeply involved in writing a book length report, called a dissertation, needed to earn his Ph.D. The report was titled "Banked Blood: A Study in Blood Preservation," and to complete the work he had to develop a blood bank at Presbyterian Hospital with the help of Dr. John Scudder.

The surgical skills Drew was developing while he worked at Presbyterian Hospital were also critical to his growth as a doctor. He would use them to become a great surgeon and eventually an inspirational teacher of other black doctors. Drew's dissertation was about as thick as a telephone book in its first draft, and it was sent back to Drew by Dr. Whipple with instructions to revise it and reduce its size. Drew accomplished this and in June 1940, Columbia University awarded him a doctor of science degree in Medicine. He was the first black American to receive his degree. (In 1908 Columbia University awarded a Ph.D. to Travis Johnson a black man from Great Britain.)[7]

Dr. Charles Drew's research and scholarship were about to catapult him into fame.

Chapter 7

Blood for Life

Blood transfusion medicine began in the United States in 1908. Dr. Alexis Carrel, a French researcher working in New York City, was called to the bedside of a newborn baby girl who was losing blood at a dangerously rapid rate. Carrel used the baby's father to transfer blood into this child. The father lay down next to his daughter and his wrist was bound to the baby's leg. Carrel cut an artery in the father's wrist which permitted blood to flow into the cut made in the baby's leg artery. The baby had been pale and was obviously losing its battle for life. Slowly the child turned pink as her father's blood flowed into her body. Dr. Carrel then clamped off both blood vessels. The baby lived and there was no damage done to the father. Carrel was widely honored for using this dramatic medical procedure as a life saving method. But blood transfusions go back much farther than 1908.

The first successful blood transfusion in the world was done far back in 1665 by British physiologist Richard Lower. He transfused blood from one dog to another and he made a vital discovery. He found that arteries spurt blood, but veins do not. (Arteries are vessels carrying blood from the heart to body tissues. Veins are vessels carrying blood from tissues to the heart.) So blood could go from a donor to a recipient by allowing it to leave the artery of a donor and enter the vein of a recipient.

In 1667, Jean Baptiste Denis infused a calf's blood into a man. The man's body rejected the blood from a different species and the experiment almost proved fatal. Denis attempted cross-species transfusions again which resulted in the deaths of some patients. Angry French citizens accused Denis of murder and in 1668, the French Parliament outlawed all blood transfusions as too dangerous to humans.

A century and a half passed before doctors once again tried to use blood transfusions to save lives. James Blundell, an English physician in London, was looking for a way to help new mothers, some of whom bled profusely giving birth and lost their lives. Blundell experimented on animals and discovered two important principles. Only human blood should be used on humans, and transfusions should be given only in case of accidental blood loss, or bleeding from illness, surgery or childbirth. Some doctors wanted to use the blood transfusions to cure madness.

In December 1818, Blundell began transfusing patients. Four of his patients died in a row, but Blundell continued. Finally he saved a bleeding woman, and during an eleven year period he transfused ten patients, saving half of them. Blundell was encouraged, but since half the patients had died, blood transfusions continued to be seen as a radical and experimental procedure. By 1875, there were records of approximately 347 transfusions throughout the world.

The process of blood transfusion was primitive and difficult. Blood was given from artery to vein through a tube or by use of a syringe. There was always danger of infection and there was no knowledge of different blood types until 1900 when Karl Landsteiner discovered the three basic blood types, A, B and C, later called O. (Later the blood type AB was added.) With the discovery of blood types and matching types to patients the success rate for transfusions increased. But, although Landsteiner had made a great contribution and was awarded the Nobel Prize for Medicine, there would be no dramatic increase in the use of blood transfusions for many years to come.

Doctors did not like to do transfusions because they were so difficult and often failed. Also, getting blood at the time a patient needed it was a problem. Even if the patient had relatives willing to donate blood, they might not have the same blood type. To meet the demand for blood for critically ill patients who had no other access to blood, doctors started putting advertisements in the newspapers seeking blood. Vagrants were paid $50 for donating blood in New York in the early 1900s. Contaminated blood from sick donors was an ever present danger. Another problem was the storage of blood. When it could not be used immediately doctors were forced to discard the precious liquid. Many years before the term blood bank became known, doctors knew they needed a place to store blood for when it was needed.

Dr. Charles Drew, in his vast dissertation, gave the Russians credit for initiating the concept of a true blood bank. Drew wrote that the Russians did the early work and assembled "most of the fundamental knowledge and the impetus for blood and plasma banks."[1]

Russian doctor Alexander Bogdanov began the practice of building transfusion centers throughout Russia where donors were paid for their blood. In 1926 he established the Central Institute on Hematology, the world's first center for transfusion research. Bogdanov conducted the early experiments on himself to learn more about the benefits and hazards of blood transfusion. In April 1928, after he had injected himself twelve times with blood during experiments, Bogdanov sickened and died from a blood infection that led to kidney failure. While he lay dying, he was dictating his symptoms to other researchers so they could learn from his experience and avoid his mistakes.[2]

Another Russian, Dr. V. N. Shamov, pioneered the practice of removing blood from a dead person and infusing it into a critically ill living person in need of blood. Drew wrote about this in his dissertation, calling attention to how Shamov's experiment proved that many parts of the body, including the blood, "retain their vitality for a varying time after the organism as a whole has ceased to function."[3] Blood from a cadaver (dead person) was used by Russian Dr. S. S. Yudin in 1930 to save the life of a young man who had cut his wrists in a suicide attempt. The man recovered quickly and following that success, Yudin was recovering blood from cadavers all over the city. Yudin tested the blood for type and made sure it was not diseased, and then he set up a small "bank" using refrigeration to store cadaver blood for when it was needed. By 1938, of the twenty-five hundred people receiving blood transfusions of cadaver blood, seven had died, another one hundred and twenty five had serious complications but survived, and the rest were very successful.

The history of blood transfusions in the United States after the dramatic Carrel experiment begins in 1925 when a group of New York doctors started an organization called The Blood Betterment Association. Their goal was to raise the standards for getting blood donations. Since most of the donated blood was coming from transients who lived on the streets and were frequently diseased, there was a serious danger of tainted blood.

Doctors were also looking into substituting blood plasma for whole blood. In 1936, Dr. John Elliott, published his findings using plasma in North Carolina. The hope was that blood plasma could be stored more easily and then reconstituted or melted back into liquid when needed.

News of the Russian experiments reached the United States in the late 1930s. Dr. Bernard Fantas of Cook County General Hospital in Chicago, Illinois established a facility in 1937 where blood donors bled into a flask. The blood was then refrigerated for later use. Fantas used the term 'blood bank' which then became the name for stored blood facilities.

In August 1939, Dr. Charles Drew and his colleague, Dr. John Scudder, opened their own experimental blood bank at Presbyterian Hospital. Drew and Scudder were leaning more toward blood plasma, rather than whole blood. It was in the field of blood plasma that Charles Drew would make his name. Drew's role in blood plasma was not in developing it, but in rounding up all the research that had been done on it, and then putting it to practical use.

By 1940, Drew and Scudder were experimenting with liquid plasma which they had received from Dr. Elliott. The clinical testing of this product was done at Presbyterian Hospital.

Drew and Scudder were already studying and measuring fluid loss and blood volume after shock in critically injured patients. Then Drew became more deeply involved in research specifically relating to blood preservation. Both Drew and Scudder had published articles for medical journals detailing their findings during research. Scudder's name usually appeared first in these jointly written articles, but, as Drew became increasingly more important, Drew's name came first in the articles. After a while, Drew was so totally immersed in this research that his name began appearing alone in the articles. Scudder praised Drew as "naturally great," and "my most brilliant pupil." He went on to call Drew "one of the great clinical scientists of the first half of the Twentieth Century."[4]

It was the Blood Transfusion Betterment Association that was contacted in 1940 when the desperate need for blood in war-ravaged Britain brought Dr. Drew into their Blood for Britain program. After his success in routing life-saving blood to Britain, Drew wrote the report that made him famous. He outlined the procedures used in the Blood for Britain project in a technical report published

January 31, 1941, by the Blood Transfusion Betterment Association. It became the standard for quickly getting blood to disaster-stricken areas all over the world.

After Britain had its own blood supply program up and operating, Drew was scheduled to return to his duties at Howard University and Freedmen's Hospital, but he asked for a three-month extension of his leave of absence.

Drew and Tracy Voorhees, legal advisers to the Blood Betterment Association, were to work together on an experiment for mass production of blood to be used by American armed forces when the United States became involved in World War II. Although the Japanese attack on Pearl Harbor would bring the United States into the war some eleven months later, most informed people believed that American involvement in the war was inevitable. Because World War II had already embroiled Europe, Asia and Africa, and the forces of Hitler's Germany were advancing, it was unlikely that the United States could be at peace much longer. And when America did get involved, rapid access to blood would be needed as military casualties mounted.

The experiment in mass blood production was sponsored by the Blood Transfusion Betterment Association, The Red Cross, and the National Research Council for Blood. The armed forces asked that these organizations undertake the program. Charles Drew was appointed assistant director under Dr. C. P. Rhoads who had directed the Blood for Britain program. Drew was also made director of the Red Cross blood bank in New York City. Drew's specific job was to oversee collection of blood for the armed forces.

On February 4, 1941, the program was under way. It differed from the Blood for Britain program in the type of blood used. Instead of using liquid plasma, the Red Cross would use dried plasma for easier storage. One thing was missing from the program, however, and that was a sense of urgency. Donors in the Blood for Britain campaign understood that critically injured people were waiting for the blood they would give and that time was important. Now, although war clouds darkened over the world and seemed likely to engulf the United States, there was still peace. Many people preferred to deny the likelihood of war. American soldiers were not taking casualties yet, which would have inspired a much greater response.

The first use of mobile units was a component of this blood drive. The trucks and ambulances began appearing at factories and department stores. Drew supervised the first mobile unit's run, going with the crew to Farmingdale, Long Island, on March 10, 1941. Although the donor turnout was less than hoped for, the experiment gave Drew and the other officials much needed practice in refining the blood collection system. They would now be ready when blood was desperately needed on battlefields from the Pacific to the European fronts.

Historians note that this program greatly increased technical know-how for the collection and storing of blood and smoothed the way for the future. Clyde Buckingham, long-time Red Cross historian, lauded the important work done by Rhoads, Drew, and others, work that was crucial to getting blood to American military casualties during the war.[5]

William DeKleine, medical director of the Red Cross in 1940–1941, said that this trial run in collecting blood started the wheels rolling "for the production of the No. 1 life-saving agent of the war . . . dried plasma."[6] The New York project, according to Robert Fletcher, an official of the Red Cross, constituted the "birth of the Blood Donor Service."[7]

Drew himself, in spite of all the praise he received, always insisted on sharing the credit with Scudder and the other men he worked with. In a letter to his mother during this hectic time, Drew described the pressures of his work and also the great satisfaction he got from seeing the different elements come smoothly together to success.[8]

When Drew finished establishing the pilot program, he prepared to return to Howard University and his work at Freedmen's Hospital. He was eager to begin what would be an extremely important part of his future work—the training of other black doctors.

Charles Drew had been away from Lenore Drew for quite some time as he worked with the Red Cross, and she was unhappy about the long separation. Since their marriage in September 1939, they had not been together very much. Lenore had returned to her mother's home to give birth to their first child, and the relationship between husband and wife was limited to letter writing. After Bebe was born, the situation did not improve much and mother and baby saw little of Drew. Drew believed his work was extremely important and he could not understand his wife's unhappiness.

In March 1941, Drew wrote Lenore a letter anticipating his return home. He admitted in the letter that up until now they had been more like courting sweethearts than husband and wife. Now that the long-distance relationship was ending and he was coming home, Drew wrote that they would discover "just what married life is like."[9] In Drew's light-hearted letter, he wondered if his wife would be able to manage having a man around the house when she had been without him for so long. He listed all the chores he could do for her once he got there, such as carrying the baby carriage upstairs, waxing the floors, taking her to the movies, and planting a flower garden.

Drew's resignation from the Red Cross was the subject of much controversy. Some people believed that he really wanted to remain in the job, but that he sensed that he would not be promoted to higher positions because he was black. Another rumor was that Drew was so offended by the Red Cross's attitude toward black blood donors that he resigned in protest. The truth was, Drew had every intention of returning to his job at Howard University at the end of the three-month period, and whatever he felt about racism in the blood bank program did not influence his decision.

When Drew left the national blood plasma project, it was running smoothly and no longer needed his hands-on direction. Drew had to fulfill his position as chief of surgery at Howard University Freedmen's Hospital or lose it. He never had any intention of losing a position in which he had invested so many of his dreams.

In April 1941, Drew took the oral certification test administered by the American Board of Surgery. This was a very challenging examination all surgeons had to take that required them to answer whatever questions were asked by a panel of experienced doctors. The examination took place at Johns Hopkins University. A famous surgeon questioned Drew on the subject of fluid balance in the human body. Drew gave such a long and complicated reply that the surgeon had to excuse himself and find more experienced doctors who could understand Drew's response. Drew had quickly advanced beyond the eminent doctors in his knowledge. This was even more evident when, six months later, Charles Drew was himself chosen to become an examiner for the American Board of Surgery. He would now judge the qualifications of other doctors. He was the first black surgeon to receive that position.

There is no question, however, that blood donor racism hurt and troubled Drew. He deplored the racist attitudes toward black donors in the United States. Throughout his professional life, Drew fought against this kind of racism. He tried to bring the light of science and reason to refute the ignorant fears people had. Some white people believed that blood from black donors was less beneficial and even dangerous to white recipients. Drew lamented that although blacks and whites "share a common blood" from the "Giver of life," he wondered if people would "ever share a common brotherhood?"[10]

In the Blood for Britain program, blood from black donors was labeled as such. But when the United States national program was initiated in 1941, the armed forces insisted that only white donors be accepted. A United States War Department edict stated "For reasons not biologically convincing but which are recognized as psychologically important in America, it is not deemed advisable to collect and mix Caucasian and Negro blood indiscriminately for later administration to the military forces."[11]

After the United States became involved in World War II, black newspapers throughout the country gave major coverage to the shameful rejection of black donors. As patriotic Americans, blacks wanted to give their blood to wounded American military men, including their own sons, brothers, and husbands, yet they were turned away. At this time the United States military was segregated along racial lines, with separate black and white units. It remained this way throughout the war. Segregation in the military did not end until 1954.

To meet the needs of black soldiers who might not want blood from white donors, the military pledged that they would look for black donors just for them. In reality this never happened. Black soldiers, when wounded, received blood from white donors. The prevailing view was that while a black donor's blood might harm a white person, a white donor's blood was good for everybody.

Drew and every other member of the scientific community realized that blood differed only in types. Race had absolutely nothing to do with it. The racial group of the donor was totally irrelevant to the quality of the blood. Incredibly, Drew himself, who had done so much to advance the blood transfusion program, was not eligible to donate blood because he was black.

Many physicians of this era, out of respect for white sensibilities, did not dispute blood donor racism. Some of Drew's black friends thought he did not do enough to fight this prejudice. Charles Drew's personality was such that he did what he thought was helpful, speaking out on the subject, but, as his wife once described it, he refused to "waste his time if he saw he was going nowhere."[12]

Drew received many letters on the subject of blood racism, some of them sincere, asking him if it was possible to transmit racial characteristics through a blood transfusion. Dr. Drew tried to answer the sincere letters with patient education. Other letters were angry and bitter. One writer said that if his white son was wounded on the battlefield and the only way to save him was to transfuse him with a black donor's blood, he would say "let him die."[13]

Drew wrote an article for the Chicago Defender in the fall of 1942 carefully refuting all the false and often absurd fears about interracial blood transfusions. He wrote that in the face of such irrational fears, "only extensive education can overcome this prejudice."[14]

Chapter 8

"My Greatest Contribution"

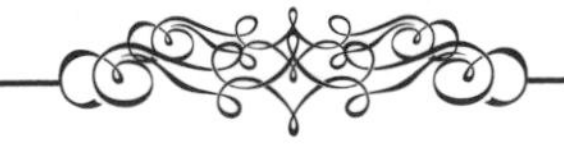

Back at Howard University in April 1941, Charles Drew was appointed professor of surgery and chief surgeon at Freedmen's Hospital. He was able to fulfill what was for him a long-standing and powerful dream—to raise the level of training for black doctors. He wanted the black doctors studying at Howard University to be as good as or better than any other doctor in the country. Charles Drew was not only breaking ground for himself, he was trying to build a generation of black doctors to be the best. In striving for this goal he constantly sought internships for black doctors across the country in white hospitals as well as training programs for his students.

Drew's work as a teacher and a mentor for younger black doctors was now more important than his research. After May 1941 to the end of his life, Drew published only four research papers. He never regretted his change in priorities. In a letter to Amherst College President Charles W. Cole, he apologized for the limited time he was devoting to research, adding, "The boys whom we are now helping to train I believe in time will constitute my greatest contribution to medicine."[1]

When Drew lectured at Howard University, the classrooms were crowded with eager listeners. When he made his rounds at Freedmen's Hospital, the residents and interns hurried after him, eager to gain his skills and inspired by his wisdom and dedication.

Drew, with his fame and brilliance, could have become a rich man, but his heart was always devoted to service. He lived on a modest teaching salary throughout his career. For example, in 1943, his gross income was $5,548 per year. It was more than the average American earned that year, $2,041, but far less than the $20,000 that he was offered to work on a large pharmaceutical company's research team.[2]

Drew hoped to train such outstanding black doctors that they could meet the most rigid demands of specialization. Then he hoped to slide them into strategic positions in white hospitals all over America. At last everyone would see that black doctors were in no way inferior to white doctors and were deserving of equal opportunities. Drew was, in the words of Dr. Samuel Bullock, a friend and surgeon at Freedmen's Hospital, "a severe teacher."[3] He was a perfectionist who expected the best from his students. He refused to lower his expectations for any black student just because that man came from a poor background. Nor would Drew lower his own standards just to push more young black doctors through the pipeline. If a particular student was having problems in class, and Drew saw promise in him, he would tutor that student to meet the high standards. But in the end each student had to rise or fall on his own merits.

Drew neither smoked nor drank liquor. He never abandoned his Bible-based upbringing, so he avoided gambling or cursing. Off-color stories and jokes offended him, and he would not permit them in his presence. Drew reprimanded his students for engaging in betting even small amounts of money. He demanded that they always be neat and professional looking.

Once, while making his rounds, Drew noticed that one of his students looked sloppy. When Drew criticized the young man's unkempt appearance, the student complained that he did not have time to take care of his appearance with all the demands of medical school. Drew told the student that he, Drew, would wash the young man's clothes and darn his socks for him, and then polish his shoes if that was the only way for him to be presentable. The student, embarrassed by the thought of Dr. Charles Drew taking care of his grooming, quickly shaped up.

Drew not only demonstrated to his students how he used various surgeon's tools, like the scalpel and clamps, but he showed them how to hold each instrument, what fingers to use, and the position of his hands throughout the procedures. Drew left nothing to chance.

When Drew spotted a particularly bright student in his class, he urged him to seek further training in the specialties beyond Howard University, as Drew himself had done when he went to Columbia. Drew was often able to get such students into advanced training programs in excellent universities.

On July 31, 1941, Lenore Drew gave birth to the couple's second child, Charlene Rosella. For Lenore, being Charles Drew's wife was not without great stresses. He was a perfectionist at home as well as at work. Just as he expected excellence from his students, he was exacting at home. Since Drew spent long hours at work, Lenore found herself raising her children almost by herself. The Drews did not take vacations because Charles did not want to be away from the hospital. The only extended family time was on Sunday afternoons when the whole family would go to Drew's mother's home in Arlington, Virginia. There would be brothers and sisters, cousins, and nieces and nephews at the family dinner, all vying for the attention of Charles Drew.

Charles and Lenore Drew lived in a large three-story house on the Howard University campus, only a few minutes from Drew's work. It was a pleasant home with fruit trees, a flower garden, and grape arbor, but it did not belong to the Drews. They would live there only as long as Drew worked for Howard University. On top of her loneliness and other worries, Lenore did not feel the security of having her own home.

The only frequent leisure activity Drew engaged in was gardening. He especially enjoyed his tall, colorful canna flowers planted in a large circle in the yard. As soon as he returned from work, he would hurry outside to see his flowers.

Charles Drew often went to medical conferences and his work schedule remained exhausting. There was very little time for Lenore and their growing family.

In spite of working so hard, Charles Drew was always taking on new challenges and in July 1941, he took on a formidable foe in his zeal to advance black doctors. He saw the American Medical Association as a serious barrier to the progress of his students.

The American Medical Association (AMA) was founded in 1847 when slavery was still the law of the land in the United States. The AMA was and remained a powerful association of physicians with the important task of setting and maintaining standards for medical schools and doctors, as well as promoting medicine and public health. Membership in the AMA was essential for a doctor to advance in his profession.

At first, the AMA banned black membership. In 1870, when changing this ban was first discussed, the national organization dodged the issue of discrimination by allowing each local AMA group to admit or refuse any doctor they chose. The southern AMA chapters refused membership to black doctors, so Charles Drew was rejected.

Charles Drew was never given membership in the AMA. He was also refused membership in the American College of Surgeons, also on the basis of his race.

In 1939, the AMA once again took up the issue of discrimination. A resolution was introduced asking that membership not be denied on the basis of race, color, or creed to any doctor, but it was voted down.

Affiliations like the AMA were not only important for giving doctors prestige and respectability, but they provided access to new advances in medicine. At their conventions, members discussed new procedures and medicines. Doctors who were excluded missed out on cutting edge technology. In order to secure membership in the AMA, Drew and other black doctors wrote letters of protest over the discriminatory practices. In spite of their efforts, it was not until after Drew's death that black doctors were finally admitted to join the Washington, D.C. branch of the AMA.

On February 14, 1944, the Drew's third child, Rhea Sylvia was born. Charles Drew was busy training his little band of students toward their final examinations, making the rounds at Freedmen's Hospital and trying to fit family responsibilities into sixteen-hour workdays. It was growing more difficult by the day for Lenore Drew, the mother of three small children, to be married to a man as relentlessly busy as Drew was.

World War II was winding down and Drew was beginning to take a stronger role in Civil Rights action.

Chapter 9

Discrimination and Dedication

Charles Drew denounced the U.S. Army's decision to ban black blood donors as a "grievous mistake, a stupid error."[1]

He also appealed for increased training of black doctors to help with the war effort. He denounced racial segregation in the military, expressing sympathy for so many black Army and Navy personnel. Though they were fighting to "rid the world of terror in far places," he said, "emancipation is not yet complete at home."[2]

In the spring of 1944, Charles Drew received the National Association for the Advancement of Colored People's Spingarn Medal, a gold medal awarded yearly to an outstanding black American. He received the honor in recognition of his work in blood research and the training of young black doctors.

In accepting the award, Drew made his first public speech denouncing blood racism. United States Senator Theodore G. Bilbo of Mississippi, a strong supporter of segregation, took note of Drew's activism. Questioning if federal funds should continue to go to Howard University with people like Drew teaching there, Bilbo blasted Drew for saying there was no difference between "colored and white people's blood."[3]

In August 1944, at a Labor Day program, Drew took part in a demonstration against segregation, something he had never done before. He called blood donor racism "a source of great damage to the morale of the Negro people."[4]

Though becoming more active in criticizing racism, Drew's main passion remained training his young doctors. Burke Syphax, one of his students who went on to teach surgery at Howard, described Drew's gift as "a knack of stimulating others." Syphax said, "He went beyond being a teacher; he was a leader of men." Syphax cited the fact that even the little black boys Drew had coached on his swimming team were making successes of their lives due to his inspiration.[5]

On October 20, 1945, the Drews welcomed their fourth child, Charles Richard Drew Jr. While Lenore cared for the new baby and the other toddlers, her husband wrote a bitter letter to the Journal of the American Medical Association calling their history of prejudice "one of the dark pages," and a "sorry record."[6] After receiving a routine reply from the AMA pointing out that the national organization was not at fault, and local groups had to be respected in their decision to bar blacks, Drew shot back a reply. He said the national organization was wrong in shirking its responsibilities in the matter.

Along with battling the AMA, Drew lent his support to many organizations he felt were helpful. He belonged to the board of trustees of the National Polio Foundation, the National Society for Crippled Children, and the American Cancer Society. He was also active in the local YMCA, recalling his own childhood when the swimming pool provided for black children gave him so much pleasure.

In December 1948, the first residents prepared by Charles Drew traveled to Johns Hopkins University to take their examinations for certification. Drew would now learn how well he had succeeded. It was one of the most tense moments in Drew's life as he awaited the medical world's verdict on the quality of these young men he had trained with such single-minded dedication.

Drew was so anxious about his students as he waited for the test results that he went down to his basement and began the hard job of dismantling an old coal bin. Only rigorous physical labor could distract his worried mind.

Drew was well aware that his students were in competition with graduates from the best white medical schools, young men who, unlike Drew's students, had grown up with many educational advantages. Still, he would not excuse them if they failed on the basis of their difficult past. He had given them his best, and he expected the best from them.

Drew finally received the phone call from Howard University president Mordecai Johnson, giving him the news he had been waiting for. Johnson first told Drew that one of his students taking the examination had come in second. Drew let out a happy shout. But then Johnson said that another of Drew's students had come in first. "First and second," Drew cried joyously, "Well, what do you know about that?"[7]

His confidence in his young doctors rewarded by such extraordinary success, Drew continued with even greater motivation. The young men trained at Howard University and Freedmen's Hospital were going on to become pioneers in many specialties of medicine, including cardiovascular surgery. Dr. Charles D. Watts, medical director for North Carolina Mutual Insurance, credited Drew with helping to prepare a whole generation of black doctors.[8] Dr. Jack White, a Drew student, became a cancer researcher. White was the seventeenth son of a poor Florida family and one of Drew's most shining successes.

Charles Drew appreciated the kindness that had been shown him through his life and delighted in the knowledge that he had helped so many young black men achieve their goals in medicine. He had the habit of sending out little thank you gifts to anyone who had shown him a kindness. When a black Texas teacher, Mrs. J. F. Bates, organized a program in Drew's honor at her school and told him about it, he warmly responded. He wrote to tell her that every worthwhile act on behalf of disadvantaged children not only helps the children and the person doing the act, it also tears down another brick in the wall of prejudice.[9]

In the summer of 1949, Drew was appointed one of four physician consultants to the Surgeon General of the United States. He was asked to go to Europe to inspect American medical facilities and to make recommendations on improvements that would make them more effective. Drew was paid to accept this job, but it also gave him a welcome chance to travel. This journey to Europe was the closest Drew would ever get to having a vacation, even though he did much important work while there. He was evaluating medical facilities but also sightseeing.

In July 1949, Drew went to Munich, Germany. He wrote Lenore that the most striking thing about the Bavarian city was block after block of rubble from World War II. In Vienna, Austria, Drew sampled classical entertainment from ballet to concerts. He noted that there was music everywhere, floating from the small cafes, from

Beethoven to American swing. Drew described Salzburg, Austria, as "shining like a jewel," and assured Lenore that he missed her very much.[10]

Lenore Drew did not reply quickly to these letters from Europe. At home, coping with four small children while her husband seemed to be having a wonderful time, she was understandably upset. While telling his wife of the beauties of Paris, Drew hastened to add that at some future time they must see Paris together.

Chapter 10

Death and Legacy

On April 1, 1950, Dr. Charles Drew was having his usual busy day that extended late into the night. He had made his rounds at Freedmen's Hospital and then he was scheduled to address a student banquet. In spite of his weariness, Drew addressed the students. Even then, he did not head home. He was planning to attend the annual free medical clinic at the John A. Andrew Memorial Hospital in Tuskegee. He never wanted to miss this event and, although he had not slept since the night before, he would not pass it up now.

Shortly after midnight, Drew and three other black physicians—Howard medical professor Samuel Bullock, and surgical interns Walter R. Johnson and John R. Ford—

all got into Bullock's 1949 Buick Roadmaster and set out from Washington, D.C., intending to drive to Tuskegee. The doctors planned to share the driving chores, going first to Atlanta where they would stay at the YMCA, then continuing the journey. It required a lot of planning for black Americans to travel in the South at that time because most hotels only rented rooms to whites.

Johnson later recalled that the four doctors began their trip in excellent spirits. They drove through the Virginia countryside under a sky ablaze with stars and illuminated by the moon. They were involved in animated conversation, sharing experiences from Freedmen's Hospital.

Drew had made this trip often but he was not at the wheel when the group left Washington. All during the night, and into the early morning, someone else drove. At about 5:30 A.M., after driving more than five hours, they reached the Virginia-North Carolina state line, and they saw a sign advertising snacks. They were all ready for refreshments so they stopped, stretched their legs, and went into the shop for doughnuts and coffee.

When the doctors resumed their trip for the next leg of the journey, which would take them to Greensboro, North Carolina, Drew took the wheel. Bullock was beside him and the two young interns were in the backseat. In spite of the rest stop they had made and the coffee they had drunk, everybody became groggy and dozed off. They were on a quiet stretch of highway on North Carolina State Route 49, north of the small village of Haw River.

Around 8 A.M., the front wheels of the car drifted off the road. Recalling the accident years later, Ford heard Bullock shout, "Hey Charlie!"[1] Startled awake by the shout and the rocking motion of the car as it went out of control, Drew grabbed the wheel and, in trying to get back on the pavement, over-corrected. The Buick twisted violently and rolled over on the soft shoulder of the road. The doors on the driver's side of the car flew open, and Drew was partially thrown out. What kept him from being thrown clear was one of his feet caught under a pedal. The Buick rolled again. This time it landed on Drew's body. The final roll of the car bounced it back upright on its four wheels, but the terrible damage had already been done.

Dr. Ford was thrown from the car when it overturned, and he suffered a broken left arm. Dr. Bullock had cuts on his hand, and Dr. Johnson was uninjured. Ford looked for Charles Drew and saw him lying on his back near the left front wheel. Johnson also saw Drew and later recalled, "He was alive; his breathing was irregular and his face was pale and contorted, as if in pain."[2] Drew was plainly in shock, a condition following loss of blood, injury to arteries, or other major trauma. As the other doctors gathered around him, they noticed a deep wound in his left leg, but it did not appear to be bleeding.

Within minutes, other motorists stopped to render assistance. Neighbors who heard the crashing sounds of the rolling car called the highway patrol. About fifteen minutes after the accident, five ambulances were on the scene. The first was probably from McClures Funeral Home (a white establishment), though there was a black-owned ambulance from Hargett and Bryant Funeral Home. Funeral homes often also operated ambulances in small towns.

Drew was placed in the ambulance, and Dr. Johnson rode with him to the hospital. Ford was taken to the same hospital by a motorist, and the highway patrol transported Bullock. At about 8:30 A.M., Drew was carried into Alamance General Hospital. Thirty to forty minutes had elapsed since the accident.

The hospital had forty-eight beds, and it was located about five miles from the accident scene. No other hospital was closer. The emergency room to which Drew was taken was on the ground floor. Duke Hospital, a much larger and more modern hospital, was about thirty-two miles from the scene of the accident. In cases of seriously injured people, the custom was to take them first to Alamance and then, once they were stabilized and judged strong enough for the long trip, they were taken to Duke. There were no specialists trained to treat brain injuries at Alamance. No black doctors were allowed to work there, but both black and white patients were frequently treated in the same emergency room.

Dr. Johnson helped the ambulance attendants wheel Charles Drew into the emergency room. Johnson recalled that at this point, Drew was still alive and gasping. The attendants checked Drew's pulse and respiration and they questioned Johnson about the accident.

Dr. George Carrington, a tall, brown-haired white man, came to the emergency room, took one look at Drew and asked, "Is that Dr. Drew?"[3] (When Drew was brought in, both Ford and Johnson immediately told the receiving personnel who the patient was.) Carrington began making emergency preparations for fluids to be gathered, and a tourniquet was placed around Drew's right arm. At this point, Dr. Johnson was sent to the waiting room while four white doctors assembled a team to work on Drew. They were Harold Kernodle, a young orthopedic surgeon; Charles Kernodle, Harold's brother and a general surgeon; Ralph Brooks, an older surgeon; and Carrington.

A white nurse on duty recalled being in the operating room ready to assist with surgery on a patient when the call came summoning her to the emergency room. She did not wait for the elevator, but ran down the steps. When she reached the emergency room she assisted Charles Drew's breathing as he lay on the operating table. Another attendant was starting an IV (placing fluids into the body through the veins). The nurse recalled that there was nothing they could do to save Drew. "He was torn up too bad," she said.[4] Though they started the fluids into Drew's body, Charles Kernodle recalled that the injuries appeared fatal from the moment the patient was brought in. Kernodle called Duke Hospital while Drew was still alive to see if doctors there could recommend any lifesaving measures. Kernodle considered sending Drew on the forty-five-minute to one-hour-long trip to Duke, but he did not think Drew would survive the journey and subjecting a dying man to this additional stress would have shown poor judgment.

The three doctors who had accompanied Drew waited for word in the hall outside the emergency room. After one hour, Harold Kernodle emerged and said, "We tried. We did the best we could."[5] Dr. Charles Drew was dead. The death certificate which was signed by Dr. Harold Kernodle gave the time of death as 10:10 A.M. The cause of death was given as injuries suffered in an automobile accident with the primary wound a brain injury, complicated by internal hemorrhage from his lungs and multiple extremities injuries.

The three black doctors stated that they believed Dr. Drew had received the best medical services that were available at that hospital at the time. They saw no evidence indicating the emergency treatment had not been acceptable.[6]

Dr. Drew's chest had been crushed in the accident when the car rolled over him and the venae cavae (the large blood vessel that drains blood into the right chamber of the heart before it is pumped to the lungs) was ruptured, which would have made a transfusion impossible.

In spite of the fact that the three black doctors with Drew had no criticism of his medical treatment, an immediate rumor started and grew to widespread proportions concerning the mistreatment of Drew. Because black patients were sometimes victims of medical neglect in the South and elsewhere in the United States, the rumors seemed reasonable. The idea that Drew, a pioneer in blood research, was denied blood when he needed it was all the more outrageous.

Dick Gregory, a popular black comedian and social commentator, told audiences all over America that "Charles Drew bled to death in an Atlanta, Georgia, hospital waiting room after an automobile accident 'cause they didn't accept blacks."[7] In truth, it was a North Carolina hospital where Drew was taken, not a Georgia hospital, and he was admitted and treated to the best of their medical ability.

Time magazine, in its March 29, 1968, issue also said that Drew was turned away from a white hospital and therefore bled to death without aid. *The New York Times* said in a June 14, 1981 story that Drew was taken to a segregated hospital that lacked the blood supplies that would have saved his life. In fact, Alamance hospital had plenty of plasma and whole blood but they could not transfuse the critically injured patient because of his chest injuries. Dr. Ford said, "All the blood in the world could not have saved him."[8]

Still, the rumor persisted and became legendary. In the 1970s the popular television comedy, *MASH*, showed an episode where the hero, Hawkeye, played by Alan Alda, explained that, although Dr. Drew invented a process for separating blood, when he needed a transfusion to save his life "the hospital wouldn't let him in. It was for whites only." So Drew "bled to death."[9] Even Whitney Young, executive director of the National Urban League (an organization founded to improve the living conditions and employment opportunities of blacks) joined in fueling the rumor. Young claimed that Drew's black colleagues had tried desperately to get Drew into the white hospital, but they were turned away. Drew then had to be taken to a more distant hospital which admitted blacks and by that time he had bled to death.[10]

Drew's daughter, Charlene Drew Jarvis, has always tried to refute the false stories. Jarvis suggests that the tragic result of the myth regarding her father's death is harmful to black people. She said that African Americans who believe the false story cite it as the reason why they will not donate blood and marrow, thus depriving many of these lifesaving gifts.[11]

In 1986, journalist Spencie Love painstakingly established that the staff at Alamance Hospital gave Drew the best care they could, that they worked with speed and dedication, and were deeply saddened that they could not save him. Drew's survival at any hospital was impossible given the level of medical skills in the early 1950s, before such dramatic advances as heart surgery and trauma units existed. Love, who earned a doctorate in history from Duke University, wrote a book detailing her research on Drew, *One Blood: The Death and Resurrection of Charles R. Drew*.

Love's book describes the pattern of neglect of other black patients and explains why the rumors about Drew were so readily accepted.

Lilliam Wiggins, a physician at Howard University, came to the Drew home on the college campus to bring Lenore Drew the news of her husband's death. Lenore recalled the moment. "Everything went cold," she said.[12] Others in the family learned of the tragedy through telephone calls from the doctors who had traveled with Drew. Several doctors from Howard University came to the Drew home to offer comfort.

At Freedmen's Hospital, as news of Drew's death spread, there was widespread grief among the medical staff. Charles Drew's body was brought home to Howard University where he lay in state at the Andrew Rankin Chapel. From Tuesday, April 4, until Wednesday morning, friends and acquaintances paid their respects at his open casket. The funeral service was conducted by the Reverend Jerry Moore at the Nineteenth Street Baptist Church at 1:00 P.M. on April 5. On the way to church the funeral procession spanned three blocks and police were at every intersection to direct traffic. The church Drew had attended as a child and adult was packed with mourners, many of them well known. Drew's old colleagues, Dr. Allen Whipple and Dr. John Scudder came from New York. Drew's casket was carried by old friends from Dunbar High School and Amherst College. Dr. Mordecai Johnson of Howard University delivered the eulogy saying that Drew had lived "a life which crowds into a handful of years significance so great that men will never be able to forget it."[13]

After the funeral, Drew was laid to rest in Lincoln Cemetery in Suitland, Maryland, two blocks from the District of Columbia line. During the ensuing years, other members of Drew's family who had been buried elsewhere were moved to Lincoln Cemetery.

Praise of Charles Drew came from Eleanor Roosevelt, widow of President Franklin Roosevelt; eminent black historian John Hope Franklin; and Pearl Buck, Pulitzer Prize-winning novelist. Congressman Hubert Humphrey of Minnesota, who later became a U.S. vice-president, entered Drew's obituary in the Congressional Record, noting that Drew was a man of "scientific devotion and integrity."[14]

Since Charles Drew always valued service over money, he never accumulated much wealth. When he died, his annual salary was only $7,000 a year, and he earned another $3,000 from private patients. At this time, skilled workers in the trades were making from $4,000 to $6,000 a year.

Drew did make contributions to an endowment fund, giving half his salary to it so that Lenore and the children would be taken care of. Lenore Drew received income from the endowment and three-fourths of Drew's salary as the widow of a Howard University professor who died during a university-related activity. Lenore Drew was able to raise her four children on this income until the youngest one reached the age of twenty-one in 1966. Since the house the family occupied was owned by Howard University and was needed for another professor on the faculty, Lenore Drew and her children had to move. Funds were raised through the Charles R. Drew Memorial Foundation to buy a home for the family.

In Drew's honor, the Drew Memorial Scholarship Fund was established at Amherst College to grant financial aid to worthy students. In New York City a public park was named for Drew and public schools all over America were named after him. In Watts, near Los Angeles, California, the Charles R. Drew Postgraduate Medical School, affiliated with the University of Southern California was created. It is a focal point for the study of health problems as they relate to black Americans.[15]

At the Clinical Center of the National Institutes of Health at Bethesda, Maryland, a portrait of Drew was unveiled October 13, 1976, becoming the first portrait of a black person to hang in the center's gallery of honors. In 1977, the Charles R. Drew Blood Center at the Red Cross building in Washington, D.C. was dedicated. A postage stamp commemorating Drew was issued on his birthday in 1981 as the fourth stamp in the Great Americans series.

On April 5, 1986, a large granite marker bearing a bronze plaque was erected on the spot near the Haw River in North Carolina on Interstate 85, between Greensboro and Durham, where Drew was fatally injured in the automobile accident.

The four Drew children grew up to be successful adults. The eldest, Roberta, became a homemaker in Columbia, Maryland. The youngest daughter, Rhea, became a lawyer, and the only son, Charles Jr., became a teacher. The middle daughter, Charlene, became a neurobiologist for the National Institutes of Health and the president of Southeastern University. Charlene Drew Jarvis also served for twenty-one years on the City Council in Washington, D.C. When she left office in January, 2001, she was described as a "masterful and tireless" politician who effectively fostered the economic development activities which have marked a rebirth of the city.[16]

Lenore Drew lived long enough to see her children prosper and to see her husband honored in many ways. She died in her home in Columbia, Maryland, in 1991 at the age of eighty.

Charles R. Drew, though he lived for only forty-five years, left behind a legacy of lifesaving techniques in the field of blood preservation and delivery. But, just as he envisioned, his greatest legacy may well be the impact he had on the other black doctors. Drew once pledged he would change the image of black doctors forever, showing the medical community they could be among the best in their profession.[17] In training a new generation of bright, skilled young black doctors, Drew succeeded admirably. "Most of the African-American surgeons trained between 1941 and 1950 in the United States were at least partially trained by Dr. Charles Drew."[18]

Charles Drew had a sense of discipleship. He wanted to inspire the next generation. "Each man's job is not just his job alone," Drew said, "but a part of the greater job whose horizons we at present can only dimly imagine."[19]

Dr. Charles R. Drew was, by all accounts, a marvelous example to those who came after him. His influence continues today in the excellence of black medicine at places like the Charles R. Drew Postgraduate Medical School and in the hearts of black children with a scientific bent, who may dream on a grander scale because he lit the way.

Chronology

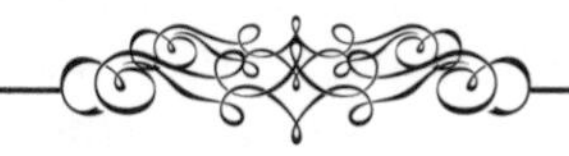

1904—Born in Washington, D.C., on June 3.

1922—Graduates from Dunbar High School.

1926—Graduates from Amherst College in Massachusetts. Becomes biology and chemistry Instructor at Morgan College in Baltimore.

1933—Graduates from McGill Medical School in Montreal, Canada with M.D. degree.

1935—Joins faculty at Howard University and resident at Freedmen's Hospital.

1938—Receives Rockefeller Fellowship to Columbia University to pursue doctorate. Works at Presbyterian Hospital.

1939—Opens experimental blood bank with Dr. John Scudder at Presbyterian Hospital. Marries Minnie Lenore Robbins.

1940—Graduates from Columbia University as Doctor of Science. *Dissertation, Banked Blood: A Study in Blood Preservation*, published. Bebe Roberta, first child, born. Directs Blood for Britain program.

1941—Returns to Howard University and Freedmen's Hospital. Passes American Board of Surgery certification at Johns Hopkins University. Charlene Rosella born July 31.

1944—Receives Spingarn Medal for medical research and leadership. Rhea Sylvia born February 14.

1945—Charles Richard Jr. born October 20.

1948—First black medical students trained by Dr. Charles Drew pass American Board of Surgery certification at Johns Hopkins University, coming in first and second.

1949—Chosen consultant to the Surgeon General of the United States to study overseas medical facilities.

1950—Dies in automobile accident on April 1, in North Carolina.

Chapter Notes

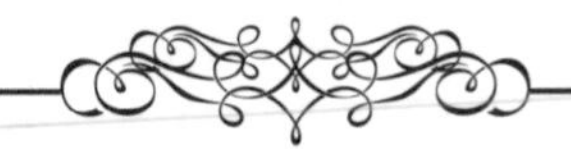

Chapter 1. Blood for Britain

1. Charles E. Wynes, *Charles Richard Drew, The Man and the Myth* (Chicago: University of Illinois Press, 1988), p. 61.

2. Douglas Starr, *Blood* (New York: Alfred A. Knopf, 1998), p. 96.

3. *African American Encyclopedia* (North Bellmore, New York: Marshall Cavendish Pub., 1993), p. 479.

4. Starr, p. 97.

5. Ibid.

6. Ibid, p. 98.

7. Columbus, Salley, *The Black 100* (New York: Citadel Press, 1993), pp. 207–209.

Chapter 2. Foggy Bottom Beginnings

1. Spencie Love, *One Blood, The Death and Resurrection of Charles R. Drew* (Chapel Hill, North Carolina: The University of North Carolina Press, 1996), p. 98.

2. Ibid, p. 99.

3. Charles E. Wynes, *Charles Richard Drew, The Man and the Myth* (Chicago: University of Illinois Press, 1988), p. 8.

4. Love, p. 104.

5. Ibid.

6. Douglas Starr, *Blood* (New York: Alfred A. Knopf, 1998), p. 96.

7. *African American Century* (New York: Simon & Schuster, Inc., 2000), p. 152.

8. Ibid.

Chapter 3. The Calling

1. Charles E. Wynes, *Charles Richard Drew, The Man and the Myth* (Chicago: University of Illinois Press, 1988), p. 15.

2. Emily J. McMurray, Ed., *Notable Twentieth Century Scientists* (New York: Gale Research, Inc., 1955), p. 523.

3. Columbus Salley, *The Black 100* (New York: Citadel Press, 1993), p. 206.

4. Spencie Love, *One Blood, The Death and Resurrection of Charles R. Drew* (Chapel Hill, North Carolina: The University of North Carolina Press, 1996), p. 109.

5. Wynes, p. 16.

Chapter 4. North to Canada

1. Michael W. Williams, Ed., *African American Encyclopedia* (North Bellmore, New York: Marshall Cavendish, 1993), p. 479.

2. Charles E. Wynes, *Charles Richard Drew, The Man and the Myth* (Chicago: University of Illinois Press, 1988), p. 18.

3. Ibid, p. 19.

4. Ibid, p. 21.

5. Spencie Love, *One Blood, the Death and Resurrection of Charles R. Drew* (Chapel Hill: North Carolina: The University of North Carolina Press, 1996), p. 116.

6. Ibid, p. 118.

Chapter 5. Howard and Freedmen's—A New Era

1. Russell L. Adams, *Great Negroes Past and Present* (Chicago: Afro-Am Publishing Company, Inc., 1969), p. 144.

2. John A. Garraty, Ed., *Encyclopedia of American Biography* (New York: Harper, 1974), p. 297.

3. Spencie Love, *One Blood, the Death and Resurrection of Charles R. Drew* (Chapel Hill, North Carolina: The University of North Carolina Press, 1996), p. 121.

4. Ibid, p. 299.

Chapter 6. Meeting Minnie Lenore Robbins

1. Charles E. Wynes, *Charles Richard Drew, The Man and the Myth* (Chicago: University of Illinois Press, 1988), p. 50.

2. Ibid, pp. 50–51.

3. Russell L. Adams, *Great Negroes, Past and Present* (Chicago: Afro-Am Publishing Co., Inc., 1969), p. 188.

4. Wynes, p. 52.

5. Spencie Love, *One Blood, The Death and Resurrection of Charles R. Drew* (Chapel Hill, North Carolina: The University of North Carolina Press, 1996), p. 123.

6. Wynes, p. 52–53.

7. Doris Simonis, Ed., *Lives and Legacies* (Phoenix, Ariz.: Oryx Press, 1999), p. 61.

Chapter 7. Blood for Life

1. Charles E. Wynes, *Charles Richard Drew, The Man and The Myth* (Chicago: University of Illinois Press, 1988), p. 45.

2. Douglas Starr, *Blood* (New York: Alfred Knopf, 1998), p. 67.

3. Wynes, p. 43.

4. Spencie Love, *One Blood, The Death and Resurrection of Charles R. Drew* (Chapel Hill, North Carolina: The University of North Carolina Press, 1996), p. 143.

5. Ibid, p. 148.

6. Ibid, pp. 148–149.

7. Ibid, p. 149.

8. Ibid, p. 150.

9. Wynes, p. 96.

10. Henry Louis Gates, Jr. and Cornel West, *The African American Century* (New York: Simon & Schuster, Inc., 2000), p. 154.

11. James Michael Brodie, *Created Equal* (New York: William Morrow, 1993), p. 141.

12. Love, p. 306.

13. Ibid, p. 307.

14. Columbus Salley, *The Black 100* (New York: Citadel Press, 1993), p. 207.

Chapter 8. "My Greatest Contribution"

1. Charles E. Wynes, *Charles Richard Drew, The Man and The Myth* (Chicago: University of Illinois Press, 1989), p. 76.

2. Spencie Love, *One Blood, The Death and Resurrection of Charles R. Drew* (Chapel Hill, North Carolina: The University of North Carolina Press, 1996), p. 310.

3. Wynes, p. 76.

Chapter 9. Discrimination and Dedication

1. Spencie Love, *One Blood, The Death and Resurrection of Charles R. Drew* (Chapel Hill, North Carolina: The University of North Carolina Press, 1996), p. 157.

2. Ibid, p. 158.

3. Ibid, p. 307.

4. Ibid, p. 159.

5. Ibid, p. 166.

6. Charles E. Wynes, *Charles Richard Drew, The Man and the Myth* (Chicago: University of Illinois Press, 1988), p. 89–90.

7. Love, p. 169.

8. Wynes, p. 78.

9. Ibid, p. 80.

10. Ibid, p. 99.

Chapter 10. Death and Legacy

1. Douglas Starr, *Blood* (New York: Alfred Knopf, 1998), p. 99.

2. Spencie Love, *One Blood, The Death and Resurrection of Charles R. Drew* (Chapel Hill, North Carolina: The University of North Carolina Press, 1996), p. 18.

3. Starr, p. 100.

4. Love, p. 21.

5. Starr, p. 100.

6. Love, p. 24.

7. Robert Siegel, "The Story of Dr. Charles Drew's Death, A Modern Myth," *All Things Considered* (NPR), February 23, 1994.

8. Starr, p. 100.

9. Love, p. 86.

10. Starr, p. 100.

11. Siegel.

12. Love, p. 28.

13. Charles E. Wynes, *Charles Richard Drew, The Man and The Myth* (Chicago: University of Illinois Press, 1988), p. 115.

14. Love, p. 30.

15. Erika Hayasaki, "Family's Role Stressed in HIV Fight," *Los Angeles Times*, July 26, 2001, p. B-4.

16. Sewall Chan, "Jarvis Takes Her Leave," *Washington Post*, January 4, 2001, p. T-3.

17. Starr, pp. 96–97.

18. James H. Kessler, et. al., Eds. *Distinguished American Scientists of the 20th Century* (Phoenix: Oryx Press, 1996), p. 74.

19. Dick Russell, *Black Genius* (New York: Carroll & Graf Publishers, 1998), p. 373.

Further Reading

Books

Cox, Clinton. *African American Healers*. New York: Wiley, 1999.

Sullivan, Otha Richard. *African American Inventors*. New York: Wiley, 1998.

Taylor-Butler, Christine. *The Circulatory System*. Danbury, Conn.: Children's Press, 2008.

Venezia , Mike. *Charles Drew: Doctor Who Got the World Pumped Up to Donate Blood*. Danbury, Conn.: Children's Press, 2008.

Whitehurst, Susan. *Dr. Charles Drew: Medical Pioneer*. North Mankato, Minn.: The Child's World, 2001.

Winner, Cherie. *Circulating Life: Blood Transfusion from Ancient Superstition to Modern Medicine.* Minneapolis, Minn.: Twenty First Century Books, 2007.

Index